FUNDAMENTAL MORAL ATTITUDES

by

DIETRICH VON HILDEBRAND

TRANSLATED FROM THE GERMAN BY
ALICE M. JOURDAIN, PH.D.

Essay Index Reprint Series

BOOKS FOR LIBRARIES PRESS
FREEPORT, NEW YORK

STANDARD BOOK NUMBER:

8369-1070-2

LIBRARY OF CONGRESS CATALOG CARD NUMBER:

77-76918

PRINTED IN THE UNITED STATES OF AMERICA

CONTENTS

One

REVERENCE

Moral values are the highest among all natural values. Goodness, purity, truthfulness, humility of man rank higher than genius, brilliancy, exuberant vitality, than the beauty of nature or of art, than the stability and power of a state. What is realized and what shines forth in an act of real forgiveness, in a noble and generous renunciation, in a burning and selfless love, is more significant and more noble, more important and more eternal than all cultural values. Positive moral values are the focus of the world; negative moral values, the greatest evil, worse than suffering, sickness, death, or the disintegration of a flourishing culture.

This fact was recognized by the great minds, such as Socrates, or Plato, who continually repeated that it is better to suffer injustice than to commit it. This pre-eminence of the moral sphere is, above all, a basic proposition of the Christian ethos.

Moral values are always personal values. They

can only inhere in man, and be realized by man. A material thing, like a stone or a house, cannot be morally good or bad, just as moral goodness is not possible to a tree or a dog. Similarly, works of the human mind (discoveries, scientific books, works of art), cannot properly be said to be the bearers of moral values; they cannot be faithful, humble and loving. They can, at the most, indirectly reflect these values, as bearing the imprint of the human mind. Man alone, as a free being, responsible for his actions and his attitudes, for his will and striving, his love and his hatred, his joy and his sorrow, and his super-actual basic attitudes, can be morally good or bad. For, far above his cultural accomplishments, rises the importance of the man's own being: a personality radiating moral values, a man who is humble, pure, truthful, honest and loving.

But, how can man participate in these moral values? Are they given to him by nature like the beauty of his face, his intelligence, or a lively temperament? No, they can only grow out of conscious, free attitudes; man himself must essentially co-operate for their realization. They can only develop through his conscious, free abandonment of himself to genuine values. In proportion to man's capacity to grasp values, in so far as he sees the fullness of the world of values with a clear and fresh vision, in so far as his abandonment to this world is pure and unconditional, will he be rich in moral values.

As long as a man blindly disregards the moral values of other persons, as long as he does not distinguish the positive value which inheres in truth, and the negative value which is proper to error, as long as he does not understand the value which inheres in the life of man, and the negative value attached to an injustice, will he be incapable of moral goodness. As long as he is only interested in the question of whether something is subjectively satisfying or not, whether it is agreeable to him or not, instead of asking whether it is something important, whether in itself it is beautiful, good, whether it should be for its own sake, in a word, whether it is something having a value—he cannot be morally good.

The soul of every morally good attitude is abandonment to that which is objectively important, is interest in a thing because it has value. Two men are, for example, witnesses of an injustice which is being inflicted upon a third person. The one who in every situation asks only whether something is agreeable

4 Fundamental Moral Attitudes

to himself or not will not be concerned about it because he calculates that no personal damage to himself can result from the other's injury. The second man, on the contrary, is willing to take suffering upon himself rather than remain disinterested in the injustice which is about to be done to the third person. For the second man, the preponderant question is not whether something is agreeable to him or not, but whether it is important in itself. The one behaves morally well, the other one morally badly, because he indifferently by-passes the question of value.

Whether one chooses or rejects something which is agreeable, but is indifferent from the point of view of value, depends upon one's own pleasure. Whether one does or does not eat an excellent meal is up to oneself. But the positive value calls for an affirmation, and the negative value for a refusal on our part. Confronted with these, the way in which one should behave is not left to one's arbitrary pleasure; instead it should be the subject of preoccupation and the right response should be given, for interest in and adequate responses on our part are due to values. Whether one does or does not help another person who is in need does not depend upon one's arbitrary pleasure; he is guilty who ignores this objective value.

Only he who understands that there exists things "important in themselves," that there are things which are beautiful and good in themselves, only the man who grasps the sublime demand of values, their call, and the duty to turn toward them and to let oneself be formed by their law, is capable of personally realizing moral values. Only the man who can see beyond his subjective horizon and who, free from pride and concupiscence, does not always ask, "what is satisfying for me?", but who leaving behind him all narrowness, abandons himself to that which is important in itself—the beautiful, the good —and subordinates himself to it, only he can become the bearer of moral values.

The capacity to grasp values, to affirm them, and to respond to them, is the foundation for realizing the moral values of man.

Now these marks can be found only in the man who possesses reverence. Reverence is *the* attitude which can be designated as the mother of all moral life, for in it man first takes a position toward the world which opens his spiritual eyes and enables him to grasp values. Consequently, in these chap-

ters which deal with moral attitudes, i.e. attitudes
which give a basis to the whole of moral life, and
are presupposed for this life, we must first of all
speak of this virtue.

The irreverent and impertinent man is the man
incapable of any abandonment or subordination of
self. He is either the slave of his pride, of that
cramping egoism which makes him a prisoner of
himself and blind to values, and leads him to ask
repeatedly: Will my prestige be increased, will my
own glory be augmented? Or he is a slave of concupiscence, one for whom everything in the world
becomes only an occasion to serve his lust. The irreverent man can never remain inwardly silent. He
never gives situations, things and persons a chance
to unfold themselves in their proper character and
value. He approaches everything in such an im-
portunate and tactless way that he observes only
himself, listens only to himself and ignores the rest
of being. He does not preserve a reverent distance
from the world.

Irreverence can be divided into two types, according to whether it is rooted in pride or in concupiscence. The first type is that of the man whose
irreverence is a fruit of his pride, that of the im-

pertinent person. He is the type of man who approaches everything with a presumptuous, sham
superiority, and never makes any effort to understand a thing "from within." He is the "know-all,"
schoolmaster type who believes that he penetrates
everything at first sight, and knows all things *ab
ovo*. He is the man for whom nothing could be
greater than himself, who never sees beyond his own
horizon, from whom the world of being hides no
secret. He is the man Shakespeare has in mind in
his *Hamlet*:

"There are more things in heaven and earth,
    Horatio,
Than are dreamt of in your philosophy."

He is the man possessed of a blighting incomprehension, without yearnings, like Famulus in Goethe's
Faust who is completely filled by "how wondrously
far he has gone." This man suspects nothing of the
breadth and depth of the world, of the mysterious
depths and the immeasurable fullness of values
which are bespoken by every ray of the sun and
every plant, and which are revealed in the innocent
laughter of a child, as well as in the repentant tears
of a sinner. The world is flattened before his im-

pertinent and stupid gaze; it becomes limited to one dimension, shallow and mute. It is evident that such a man is blind to values. He passes through the world with a blighting incomprehension.

The other type of man who lacks reverence, the blunt, concupiscent man, is equally blind to values. He limits his interest to one thing only: whether something is agreeable to him or not, whether it offers him satisfaction, whether or not it can be of any use to him. He sees in all things only that segment which is related to his accidental, immediate interest. Every being is, for him, but a means to his own selfish aim. He drags himself about eternally in the circle of his narrowness, and never succeeds in emerging from himself. Consequently, he also does not know the true and deep happiness which can only flow from abandonment to true values, out of contact with what is in itself good and beautiful. He does not approach being as does the first type in an impertinent way, but he is equally closed up within himself, and does not preserve that distance toward being required by reverence; he overlooks all things and seeks only that which is momentarily useful and expedient to him. Similarly, he can never be inwardly silent, or open his

spiritual self to the influence of being and allow
himself to receive the joy that values give. He
is also, as it were, in a perpetual egospasm. His
look falls on all things flatly, "from the outside,"
without comprehension for the true meaning and
value of an object. He also is shortsighted, and
comes too close to all things, so that he does not
give them a chance to reveal their true essence. He
fails to leave to any being the "space" which it
needs to unfold itself fully and in its proper mode.
This man also is blind to values, and to him again
the world refuses to reveal its breadth, depth and
height.

The man possessing reverence approaches the
world in a completely different way. He is free
from this egospasm, from pride and concupiscence.
He does not fill the world with his own ego, but
leaves to being the space which it needs in order to
unfold itself. He understands the dignity and
nobility of being as such, the value which it already
possesses in its opposition to mere nothingness.
Thus there is a value inherent in every stone, in a
drop of water, in a blade of grass, precisely as
being, as an entity which possesses its own being,
which is such and not otherwise. In contradistinction

to a fantasy or a sheer semblance, it is something independent of the person considering it, and is something withdrawn from his arbitrary will. Hence each of these things has the quite general value of existence.

Because of this autonomy, being is never a *mere* means for the reverent man and his accidental egoistic aims. It is never merely something which he can use, but he takes it seriously in itself; he leaves it the necessary space for its proper unfolding. Confronted with being, the reverent man remains silent in order to give it an opportunity to speak. The man who possesses reverence knows that the world of being is greater than he is, that he is not the Lord who can do with things as He likes, and that he must learn from being, not the other way around.

This responsive attitude to the value of being is pervaded by the disposition to recognize something superior to one's arbitrary pleasure and will, and to be ready to subordinate and abandon oneself. It enables the spiritual eye to see the deeper nature of every being. It leaves to being the possibility of unveiling its essence, and makes a man capable of grasping values. To whom will the sublime beauty

of a sunset or a ninth symphony of Beethoven reveal itself, but to him who approaches it reverently
and unlocks his heart to it? To whom will the mystery which lies in life and manifests itself in every
plant reveal itself in its full splendor, but to him
who contemplates it reverently? But he who sees in
it only a means of subsistence or of earning money,
i.e. something which can be used or employed,
will not discover the meaning, structure and significance of the world in its beauty and hidden dignity.

Reverence is the indispensable presupposition
for all deep knowledge—above all, for the capacity
to grasp values. All capacity to be made happy and
uplifted by values, all sanctioned abandonment to
values, all submission to their majesty, presupposes reverence. In reverence the person takes into
account the sublimity of the world of values—in it
is to be found that upward look toward that world,
that respect for the objective and valid demands immanent to the values which, independently of the
arbitrary will and wishes of men, call for an adequate response.

Reverence is the presupposition for every response to value, every abandonment to something
important, and it is, at the same time, an essential

element of such response to value. Each time one gives oneself to the good and beautiful, each time one conforms to the inner law of value, the basic attitude of reverence is implied. This can be verified by examining moral attitudes on the different levels of life.

The fundamental attitude of reverence is the basis for all moral conduct toward our fellowmen and toward ourselves. Only to the man possessing reverence is revealed the full grandeur and depth of the values which inhere in every man as a spiritual person. The spiritual person as a conscious, free being, as a being who alone, among all the entities known to us, is capable of knowing and grasping the rest of being, and of taking a meaningful position toward it, can only be comprehended by a reverent mind. A being who is able and destined to realize in himself a rich world of values, to become a vessel of goodness, purity, and humility—this is a person. How could one really love another person, how could he make sacrifices for him, if he senses nothing of the preciousness and plenitude which is potentially enclosed in man's soul, if he has no reverence for this being?

The basic attitude of reverence is the presupposition for every true love, above all, the love of neighbor, because it alone opens our eyes to the value of men as spiritual persons, and because, without this awareness, no love is possible. Reverence for the beloved one is also an essential element of every love. To give attention to the specific meaning and value of his individuality, to display consideration toward him, instead of forcing our wishes on him, is part of reverence. It is from reverence that there flows the willingness of a lover to grant the beloved the spiritual "space" needed to freely express his own individuality. All these elements of every true love flow from reverence. What would mother love be without reverence for the growing being, for all the possibilities of values which yet lie dormant, for the preciousness of the child's soul?

A similar reverence is evident in justice toward others, in consideration for the rights of another, for the liberty of another's decisions, in limiting one's own lust for power, and in all understanding of another's rights. Reverence for our neighbors is the basis for all true community life, for the right approach to marriage, the family, the nation, the state, humanity, for respect of legitimate authority, for the fulfillment of moral duties toward the community as a whole and toward the individual members of the community. The irreverent man splits apart and disintegrates the community.

But reverence is also the soul of the correct attitude in other domains, such as purity. Reverence for the mystery of the marital union, for the depth and tenderness and the decisive and lasting validity of this most intimate abandonment of self, are the presuppositions for purity. First of all, reverence assures an understanding of this sphere; it shows us how horrible is every illicit approach to this mysterious domain, since such an illicit approach desecrates us and involves so serious a debasement of our dignity and that of others. Reverence for the wonder of the coming into being of a new life out of the closest union of love of two people is the basis for the horror of every criminal, artificial and irreverent act destroying this mysterious bond which exists between love and the coming into being of new men.

Wherever we look, we see reverence to be the basis and at the same time an essential element of moral life and moral values. Without a fundamental attitude of reverence, no true love, no justice, no kindliness, no self-development, no purity, no truthfulness, are possible; above all, without reverence, the dimension of depth is completely excluded. The irreverent person is himself flat and shallow, for he fails to understand the depth of being, since for him there is no world beyond and above that which is visibly palpable. Only to the man possessing reverence does the world of religion open itself; only to him will the world as a whole reveal its meaning and value. So reverence as a basic moral attitude stands at the beginning of all religion. It is the basis for the right attitude of men toward themselves, their neighbors, to every level of being, and above all to God.

Two

FAITHFULNESS

Among the attitudes of man which are basic for his whole moral life, faithfulness is ranked next to reverence. One can speak of faithfulness in a narrow sense and in a large one. We have the narrow sense in mind when we speak of fidelity toward men, such as fidelity to a friend, marital fidelity, fidelity to one's country or to oneself.

This type of fidelity throws into relief the other type. I refer here to the continuity which first gives to a man's life its inner consistency, its inner unity. The building up of one's personality is only possible if one holds firmly to those truths and values which one has already discovered.

The course of a man's life contains a continual rhythmical replacement of one impression, one act, one decision by another and different impression, act or decision. We are unable to ponder over one thought for a long time and to keep our attention on one point for very long. Just as in the biological

16

realm, hunger and satiety, fatigue and renewed
strength succeed one another, so a certain rhythmical
change is proper to the course of our spiritual life.
Just as the various impressions which affect us give
place to one another, and the stream of events offers
to our mind a great variety of objects, so our attention cannot long remain focused on any one
object with the same intensity. A movement from
one subject to another is therefore proper to our
thought, as well as to our feeling and will. Even in
the case of a very blissful experience, such as the
long-desired meeting with a beloved person, we are
unable to dwell permanently in this joyous experience. The rhythm of our inner life forces us to leave
the full presence of a great joy and to turn our attention in another direction and to register different
experiences.

But—and this must be stressed—the same man
has different levels of depth. The psychical life of
man is not restricted to the level on which this continual change unfolds itself; it is not restricted to
the level of our express attention, of our present
consciousness. While we proceed to another impression and give our attention to another mental
object, the preceding impression or object does not

vanish, but will, according to its significance, be retained in a deeper level, and will continue to live at that level. Memory is an expression of this capacity of the soul for superactual life, and this continuity is seen in our capacity to remember, to connect past and present.

Above all we see this continuity in the super-actual survival of our attitudes toward the world, toward fundamental truths and values, which remain unchanged even though our present attention is turned in a completely different direction. Thus, for example, joy caused by some happy event continues to "live" in the depth of our souls and colors everything which we do, colors all our tasks of the moment, and colors our approach to all those things with which we are expressly concerned. So also our love for a beloved person remains living in the depth of our souls, even though we are occupied by work, and it constitutes a sort of background before which different events run their course. Without this capacity for continuity, man would have no inner unity; he would be but a bundle of interwoven impressions and experiences. If one impression merely took the place of the preceding one, if the past should indiscriminately vanish, the

inner life of man would be senseless and shallow;
any building up, any development would be impossible. Above all there would be no personality.

Even though this capacity of retaining impressions and attitudes in a superactual way, without
which the individual life of a spiritual person is
impossible, is a capacity common to every man, yet
the degree to which a given individual possesses
this inner continuous coherence is very different in
each case. We say of many men that they live in
the moment only; the present instant has such
power over them that the past, even though its content be deeper and more important, vanishes before
the insistent clamor of the present.

Men differ very much from each other in this
regard. Some of them live exclusively on the exterior level of their present consciousness, so that
one experience follows another without any relation
to the one preceding. We could call such men
"butterflies." Others, on the contrary, also live in
the deeper level of their being. In them nothing
important is sacrificed just because it is no longer
present, but it becomes the unalterable possession
of the man, according to its degree of importance,
and the new meaningful experiences organically

unite themselves with it. The last type alone can be
said to have "personality." Only in them can an
inner spiritual plenitude be constituted.

How many people there are who are never lastingly influenced by great works of art, or by delight
in beautiful landscapes, or by contact with great
personalities? The momentary impression may be
strong but it strikes no deep root in them; it is not
firmly held in their superactual life but disappears
as soon as another impression makes its appearance. These men are like a sieve through which
everything runs. Though they can be good, kindly
and honest, they cleave to a childish, unconscious
position; they have no depth. They elude one's
grasp, they are incapable of having deep relationships with other people because they are capable of
no permanent relationship with anything. These
men do not know responsibility because they know
no lasting bond, because with them one day does
not reach into the next one. Even though their impressions are strong, they do not penetrate down
to the deepest level in which we find those attitudes
which are over and above the changes of the
moment. These people honestly promise something
one moment, and in the next it has completely

disappeared from their memory. They make resolutions under a strong impression, but the next
impression blows them away. They are so impres-
sionable, that they are always held at the superficial
level of their present consciousness. For these
people, weight and value are not the preponderant
factors determining their interest in things, but only
the liveliness of the impression created by the
actual presence of these things. What makes an
impression upon them is the general advantage of
"liveliness" which present impressions or situations
have over those of the past.

There are two types of inconstant men. In the
one, nothing ever truly penetrates to their deeper
center. This deeper center, so to speak, remains
void in them; they know only the strata of present
consciousness. These men are at the same time
superficial, deprived of profound life, and of any
sort of inner "firmness." They are like quicksand
which yields without any resistance. If you seek in
such men a permanent center upon which you can
depend and rely, then you really snatch at the void.
Of course, in a healthy man this is not absolutely
and completely the case; a man who, in a literal
sense, would be completely of this character would

be a psychopath. But we often meet people whose lives, at least to a certain extent, unfold themselves in such a manner, although we could not therefore call them psychotic.

In the second type, we have to deal with men who actually do have deep impressions, in whose deeper strata much really does take root. Their deeper consciousness is therefore not void; they have created in themselves a firm, lasting center. But they are so imprisoned in the present moment that that which lies in their deeper strata is unable to carry its true weight; it cannot hold its ground against the power of the momentary impression. Only when the present, lively impression fades away, can the content of the deeper strata again come to light. Such men could, for example, very well nourish a deep, lasting love for another person, but a momentary situation, if it happens to be powerful, vivid and appealing, would capture them to such an extent that the beloved one would be almost forgotten. Then they say and do things which contradict the genuine and living love hidden in the depths of their souls. Such people are continually in danger of becoming traitors to themselves or to

others. For such persons, the one present, merely because he is present, has always the advantage over
the absent. This is the case even when the absent person is, on the whole, dearer to them, and in the long
run, plays a more important role. Suppose they
have, for example, received a deep impression from
a work of art: a lasting relation to this work of art
has constituted itself in the depths of their souls.
Nevertheless, new powerful impressions take hold
of them to such an extent, that the prior impression
is not firmly held in the new situation, and as a result one sees no trace of the first impression as long
as the new one lasts. Later, when the immersing
effect of the new situation has worn off, the old one,
in itself deeper, re-enters into possession of its
rightful place and authority.

In contradistinction to these two types, the per-
severing man holds on to everything which has revealed itself to him as a true genuine value. The
advantage of liveliness which the present possesses
over the past, has no power over his life when com-
pared to the inner weight of deep truths which he
has once recognized, and of values which he has
once grasped. The importance of the role played by

a given thing in his present consciousness is exclusively determined by the height of its value, and in no way by its mere presence.

Such men are, consequently, protected from the tyranny of fashion. A thing never makes a deep impression upon them merely because it is modern, because it is momentarily "in the air," but only because it has a value, because it is beautiful, good and true. As a matter of fact, these persons consider that which is more important and has a higher value as itself the more "up to date." Objects endowed with values never grow old for them, even if their concrete existence ceased long ago. The lives of these men are meaningfully integrated, and in their course reflects the objective gradation of values. While the inconstant man is a prey to accidental impressions and situations, the constant man dominates his own impressions. Such men alone understand the sublime pre-eminence of values over any mere dimension of time, the unchanging and unfading character of values and truth. They understand that an important truth is not less interesting and less worthy of concern because we have known it for a long time. They understand, above all, that the obligation to respond to a good possessing a

179.9 V895f

C. 1

value is not limited to the moment in which it is grasped.

Only the man who is constant really grasps the demands of the world of values; only he is capable of the response to value which is due to objective values. A proper response to values is lasting, independent of the charm of novelty, and of the attractive force represented by the mere presence of a thing. He alone for whom values never lose their efficacy and charm, once they have been revealed to him, and who never lets a truth which he has grasped drop into oblivion will really do justice to the proper character of the world of truth and values; for he alone is capable of remaining faithful to objects possessing value.

This constancy or fidelity in the true sense of the word is, as we see, a fundamental moral attitude of man. It is a necessary consequence of all true understanding of values, and it is a component element of every true response to values, and consequently of the whole moral life. Only the constant response to values, the response which clings to a thing possessing a value, whether that thing is actually present or not, is a developed, a morally mature and fully conscious response to value. Only a man who responds in this way is truly morally awakened; he alone is reliable, he alone feels himself to be responsible for that which he has done in other situations, he alone is capable of a true contrition for previous misdeeds. In him alone all true obligations will dominate every situation of his life. He alone will stand firm in trials. For the light of values will shine for him even in the humdrum situations of workaday life; yes, even at the moments of temptation. It is so because this man lives from the depth, and masters every moment *from* the depth. The more faithful, the more constant a man is, the richer and more substantial will he be, the more capable of becoming a vessel of moral values, a being in whom purity, justice, humility, love and goodness will dwell lastingly and will radiate from him to the world about him.

Were we to examine the different levels of life, we would find over and over again the basic significance of faithfulness in this larger sense. The basic attitude of constancy is a general presupposition for all spiritual growth of the person, and above all for every moral development and every moral progress. How can a man grow spiritually who does not firmly adhere to all the values which have been revealed to him, and for whom these values do not become a lasting possession? How could one who is dominated by short-lived momentary impressions ever succeed in a gradual development of his own moral structure?

When we have to deal with the type of radical inconstancy we first mentioned in this chapter, we see that nothing at all reaches down into such a person's deeper strata. Such men are inwardly dead; their personality lacks a lasting center. In men of the second type, there is lacking the possibility of a real formation of the course of life, for the values they once grasped, and which should be a permanent possession of their souls, have disappeared from their lives. They cannot therefore mold new impression by such values. What is the use of the best education if this constancy is missing? What is the use of the most pressing exhortations, of the most vivid revelation of values, if values once grasped remain either without any permanent roots or if they slumber in our souls? As surprising as it may sound, inconstant people never change themselves. They retain the faults and features which they have inherited from their nature, but they acquire no moral values. Even though they really

do for a moment recognize their faults, and form
the best resolutions, their inconstancy prevents any
lasting moral improvement. Even when their will
is good, education will have no lasting effect upon
them. Not because they close themselves up, like
the man who is victim of a cramping pride and to
whom therefore the influence of values cannot penetrate, but because they give too much weight to
every fleeting impression, and they are thus unable
to retain what they have acquired.

All self-education presupposes this attitude of
constancy. The constant man alone will be able to
assimilate contradictory impressions, so as to draw
that which is good out of each. He will learn from
every situation of life and will grow in every situation, for in him the measure of genuine values
remains alive; while the inconstant man yields now
to one, now to another impression, and becomes so
entirely a prey of each that in the depth of his soul
everything passes on more or less without leaving
a trace. This gradually withers his comprehension
of values, and his susceptibility to their influence.
The constant man alone will prefer what is more important to what is less so, what is more valuable to
the less, while the unstable person will at best re-

spond indiscriminately to all values, recognizing
no hierarchy in them. Nothing is, in fact, more important for moral growth, for the very moral life of
a person, than consideration for the objective hierarchy of values, and the capacity to give priority to
that which ontologically is objectively higher.

The fundamental attitude of fidelity is also the
presupposition for reliability in every moral trial.
How can he keep a promise or stand the test in a
battle of ideas, who lives only in the present
moment, in whom the past, present and future do
not form any significant unity? How can one rely
upon such an inconstant person? The faithful man
alone can inspire that confidence which forms the
basis of any community. He alone possesses the
high moral value of stability, reliability and trust-
worthiness.

But constancy is also a condition for any confidence on the part of the person himself and above
all for heroic faith. The unstable man is not only
undeserving of confidence, but he himself will be
incapable of a firm, unshakable confidence either
in other men, in truth, or in God Himself. For such
a man lacks the strength to nourish his soul upon a
value once discovered. Therefore when night and

obscurity surround him, or when other strong impressions assail him, he loses faith. It is no accident that in Latin the word *fides* means both fidelity and faith. For constancy is an essential constituent of all capacity to believe, and consequently of all religion.

The eminent importance of faithfulness will stand out in a special way against the background of human relationships. (Here faithfulness is taken in its narrow sense, i.e. fidelity.) For what is love without fidelity? In the ultimate analysis, it is nothing but a lie. For the deepest meaning of every love, the inner "word" uttered in love, is the interior orientation toward and giving of oneself to the beloved, a giving which knows no time limit. No fluctuation in the course of life can shatter it. Only a deep change in the beloved person can affect our love if it be true love. A man who would say: "I love you now, but how long it will last, I cannot tell," does not truly love; he does not even suspect the very nature of love. Faithfulness is so essentially one with love, that everyone, at least as long as he loves, must consider his devotion an undying devotion. This holds good for every love, for parental and filial love, for friendship and for spousal love. The deeper a

love, the more it is pervaded by fidelity. It is precisely in this faithfulness that we find the specific
moral splendor, the chaste beauty of love. The
especially touching element of love, as expressed
so uniquely in Beethoven's *Fidelio*, is essentially
tied up with fidelity. The unalterable fidelity of a
mother's love, the victorious faithfulness of a
friend, possess a specific moral beauty which
touches the man whose heart is opened to values.
Faithfulness is at the heart of every true and deep
love. It is immanent to its very nature.

On the other hand, what is more base or more re-
pulsive than outspoken unfaithfulness, that radical
opposition to fidelity, which is far worse than mere
inconstancy. What a heinous moral stain marks the
traitor who by infidelity pierces the very heart
which has confidently opened itself to him, and
offers itself unprotected to him. He who is unfaith-
ful in his basic attitudes is a Judas to the world of
values.

There are people to whom fidelity appears in the
light of a mere bourgeois virtue, a mere correctness,
a technical loyalty. In the opinion of such people
the man who is great, highly gifted and freed from
"petty conventions," has no concern with it. This is

a senseless misunderstanding of the true nature of
fidelity. It is true that too strong an emphasis on
one's own fidelity may create a painful impression.
It is true that it is possible to give a certain harmless, good-natured cheap imitation of fidelity. The
fact remains that true faithfulness is an indispensable element of all moral greatness, of all depth and
strength of personality.

Fidelity is opposed to mere bourgeois loyalty, or
to a pure clinging to habit. It would be an error to
believe that fidelity is the mere result of a lazy
temperament, and inconstancy the result of a spon-
taneous and vivacious one. No, this virtue is a free,
meaningful response to the world of truth and of
values, to the unchangeable and intrinsic importance, to the real demands, of that world. Without
this basic attitude of fidelity, no culture, no progress
in knowledge, no community, above all no moral
personality, no moral growth, no substantial, inwardly unified spiritual life, no true love, are possible. This basic significance of fidelity, in the
larger sense, must penetrate to the heart of every
relationship, if it is not to be judged, *ab ovo*, as a
failure.

Three

AWARENESS OF RESPONSIBILITY

When we call someone a "morally conscious" man, and another man a "morally unconscious" one, we have in mind a difference which is decisive from the ethical point of view. The unconscious man drifts through life; of course, he grasps certain values, and responds to them, but this process goes on in a manner that is deprived of an ultimate *awakedness* and of an explicit character. His grasp of values remains more or less accidental. Above all, his life, on the whole, is not consciously and expressly lived under the awful sword of good and evil. Even when, at a given moment, he rejects something bad and affirms something good, at heart this attitude is rather an affirmation of his own temperament than a really enlightened cooperation with the implacable demands of values, and conformity to those demands.

The unconscious man behaves according to the impulses of his nature; he has not yet discovered

within himself the capacity to direct himself freely
toward the objective demands of the world of values
independently of what is or is not congenial to his
nature. He is unaware of this capacity freely to approve or disavow impulses arising from his own
nature, according to whether they are or are not in
conformity with the world of values. Unconscious
men are not awakened to the specifically *moral* pre-
rogative of the spiritual person either to freely
approve or to disavow; they make no use of it. Consequently, they ignore the necessity for conscious
effort to develop and improve their moral stature.
In their lives we find no moral self-education. This
moral sluggishness is an obstacle to the formation
of a moral personality. Moral consciousness and
moral awakedness are indispensable presuppositions for a real grasp of values, for true responses
to values and consequently for the possession of
moral values. The morally unconscious man can
be good, faithful, just, and a friend of truth, but
only in the sense that he is a pale reflection of these
virtues. His goodness, fidelity, justice and truthfulness lack the specific beauty of moral excellence, a
full and free turning to values, a submission to their
sovereign majesty, and real subordination to their

eternal laws. The accidental character of such a
man's virtues and the incomplete character of his
responses deprives them of their true moral core.
They are moral virtues whose soul is deprived of
its ultimate, free, meaningful life.

Reverence and that true fidelity, which we have
called constancy, are closely related to this moral
awakedness. Moreover, they can only fully unfold
themselves in a morally conscious man. This moral
awakedness is also the soul of the fundamental
moral attitude which we have called "awareness of
responsibility." Only the man with this consciousness of responsibility can justly appreciate the im-
pact of the demands of the world of values. He
grasps not only the splendor, the inner beauty and
majesty of the world of values, but also the sovereignty over us which is objectively due to this world.
He understands the implacable earnestness of their
demands, he experiences their personal call on us.
He perceives the commands and the prohibitions
which issue from values. He possesses that awakedness toward the world of values which places his life
under its sword of justice, which makes him at every
moment aware of his own position and duties in the
cosmos, and makes him realize clearly that he is not

his own master. He knows that he cannot act freely according to his arbitrary pleasure, that he is not his own judge, but that he must render an account to Someone Who is higher than he is.

The very opposite of the man who is conscious of his responses, is the heedless and thoughtless man. The most radical type in this category is represented by the man who does not in the least concern himself with the world of values, but only with what is subjectively satisfying to him. He is the coarse man subject to his own desires who blindly by-passes all values and for whom the whole world offers only an occasion to secure more pleasure; this is the same type of man we have designated earlier as one who lacks reverence. He lives in darkness, almost as an animal, and casts the world of values completely aside. He is not concerned with either good or evil, and takes no notice of the importance of the demands of the world of values, or of the sword of justice which hangs over his head. Although he may pursue his quest of pleasure and enjoyment with remarkable cleverness and care, he is possessed by an ultimate, a terrible thoughtlessness. It is obvious that this man who is never touched by values, who knows no abandonment to them, is completely irresponsible.

Completely different from this totally corrupted type in whom no moral value can flower at all, is the morally unconscious man of whom we have spoken above, who really *does* grasp values, is affected by them, and sometimes even conforms to them, but who has not a full understanding of them, since he is deprived of a conscious and explicit awareness. He is also filled with a deep thoughtlessness, with a lack of realization of the ultimate importance of the world of values and its demands. He can be good natured, amiable, generous, ready to help, but all this without an ultimate attainment of moral excellence. This man also does not possess a consciousness of responsibility. In the different situations of life he does not seek a really clear and unequivocal decision on the question of value; to say "yes" or "no," it suffices for him to have an approximate impression of what is good or evil, what is beautiful or ugly. This is understandable; for he does not consider the specific, objective nature of the value and its demand, but only whether a given attitude suits him or not, whether or not it is in inner conformity to his temperament. Consequently, his responses will be thoughtless, deprived of unequivocal clarity of vision with regard to the values at stake in any concrete situation.

Finally, there exists a type of thoughtless man who makes a conscious moral effort, but who, on account of a certain superficiality and frivolity in his nature does not consider it necessary in making his decisions to have a clear and precise notion of the value in question. He does not exert himself to work out a clear idea of the question of value in a given case. He will make decisions in serious cases on the pure appearance of good or evil. What public opinion says, what is advised by an acquaintance, what appears to him through convention, as correct, suffices for him to take a position in a given case. He fails to understand that before making a decision the importance of the question of whether or not an adequate response has been given to values imperatively obliges us to reach a *real* and clear understanding regarding the demands of those values. The thoughtlessness of such men lies in the fact that they do not take the question of value seriously enough; that in spite of their good will, they reach an affirmative or negative decision without having truly harkened to the voice of values, without taking the trouble to really examine what is due to values.

Through this lack of a sense of responsibility, the life of such a man actually becomes a sort of game, played out on the surface. So long as this attitude is dominant, the man in question remains immature and childish. This attitude is also proper to the typically inconstant man, of whom we have spoken in a previous chapter, who lives only in the present moment, and who cannot retain the acquisitions of his deeper experience because of the influence of those which are present. The man lacking in a sense of responsibility also responds too quickly, without taking the trouble to test new experiences against the background of truths he has already discovered. The morally negative attitude of this lack of a sense of responsibility is particularly striking when we are dealing not only with an interior attitude, but with an exterior transient action. Obviously, every "yes" or "no" which is uttered in response to values, is a part of reality, and therefore carries the whole decisive import of reality as opposed to the mere possibilities which may present themselves to our imagination. Here again, there yawns an abyss between a tendency arising in us and the inner "yes" or "no" of a fully conscious response. In every purely inner decision that we reach, in every enthusiasm or indignation freely sanctioned by us there lies something which we cannot undo. But an action which intervenes in the exterior world is still more irrevocable if the status *ante quo* cannot be restored. For in the case of inward attitudes, by means of an inner revocation of the past through genuine contrition, we can at least erase an essential element of what has really taken place. But he who has neglected a once-given opportunity in the sphere of external action cannot undo what he has done; he who has failed to save another man whose life is in danger cannot resuscitate him.

In lack of responsibility, in thoughtlessness, there is also evident a lack of respect for reality, for the import of something which has once been brought into existence. There is as well a blighting lack of comprehension of this irrevocable seriousness and

"This is the curse of every evil deed,
That, propagating still, it brings forth evil."

SCHILLER

The thoughtless man is frightened when he realizes what he has done. His guilty deed is not the result of bad intention, but of a general and blighting lack of comprehension of the seriousness and importance of reality. Lack of understanding of the seriousness of the demands of values, failure to respond to this aspect of the world of values, induces in him a misunderstanding of the import of "reality." It is quite understandable that from a frivolous attitude toward reality there will issue decisions formed without sufficient understanding of the demands that emanate from values. Moreover, we find such a man disinterested in the consequences of an action; his attitude is to consider only the present moment. Of course, certain consequences are not always to be foreseen, and certain demands of values are such that they, so to speak, themselves assume the responsibility of possible consequences. But in the majority of cases, we should, before making a decision, examine whether the consequences of our action, as far as they can be foreseen and still more if they are inevitable, are in themselves good or bad. Otherwise, a true interest in values would be lacking.

The man who is aware of his responsibility,

on the other hand, understands the full seriousness
of the world of values and its demands, and takes
these demands into account. He grasps the entire
seriousness and irrevocable character of reality
inherent in every decision. Insofar as is at all possible in a given situation, he makes a decision, he
takes his position, only when the question of value
is unequivocally clear to him. His life bears the seal
of awakedness, of earnestness, instead of frivolity,
of manliness instead of childishness. This does not
mean that the man aware of his responsibilities
must be an ultra-cautious person, who endlessly
hesitates and endlessly deliberates before taking a
stand or making a decision. In a given situation he
can just as well make a choice without further
deliberation, if the value at stake reveals itself at
first sight, in unmistakable clarity. The question of
whether a man is aware of his responsibility or not
does not depend upon whether the basis of his decision is an immediate intuition of the value or
whether it is reached by deliberation. What matters
exclusively is whether the value is or is not unequivocally clear to him.

What decides the specific nature of the consciously awakened man is not the difference be-

tween an ultra-cautious, hesitating and slow temperament as opposed to an energetic and prompt one. No, an awakened man will act either cautiously or promptly according to whether, at first sight, he is or is not unequivocally clear concerning the value at stake. It is not his temperament but the degree to which the values or negative values and their demands are objectively lucid to him which will lead him in one case to take an immediate and apparently impulsive position, while in another, to examine the situation with concern and delibera- tion. Thanks to his awakedness and reverence for the world of values and the importance of reality, he understands that before making a decision he is called upon to obtain the greatest possible evidence concerning the values at stake.

The man who is truly and consciously aware of his responsibility is, however, far from placing stubborn reliance upon his own insight. He has nothing in common with the so-called proud and self-assured man, who believes that he owes it to himself to base all decisions exclusively upon his own insight. The man who is truly and consciously aware of his responsibility has nothing of this cramping egotism and this moral pride; he is, on the contrary, exclusively concerned with fulfilling the objective demands of the world of values. Such a man is also aware of the limits of his own ability and capacity to grasp values, and accordingly allows himself to be guided by the clear insight of someone he knows to be morally superior and to have a deeper grasp of values, rather than preferring to follow a vague impression which his own insight gives him of a certain situation. First of all, he will be guided by the commandments of a true authority. But he himself must first be convinced beyond doubt of the superiority of his adviser in the understanding of morally relevant values, and he must clearly understand the legitimate nature of that adviser's authority. He will not allow pure suggestion to have any influence upon his decisions. He will not let himself be talked into anything nor will he be bluffed by others; above all, he will not allow persons who possess a dynamic temperament and whose superiority does not lie within the moral sphere to impose their ideas and advice upon him, to intimidate him or to shake his decision.

Awareness of responsibility is an indispensable presupposition for any true moral life. By means of this basic attitude of awakedness, everything in

a man assumes its full importance, its true depth.
But one should not confuse this awareness of responsibility with a feeling of moral self-importance
or over-estimation of one's own role in the world.
The responsible man must be completely inspired
by the world of values and their demands; he must
reverently harken to that which is objectively right,
good and beautiful; he must be inwardly free to
follow always and everywhere the call of values.
This awareness of responsibility has nothing to do
with the excessive anxiety of scrupulous persons.
The scrupulous man constantly scrutinizes what he
is morally obliged to do; but this does not mean that
his interest in values is an extraordinary one. No,
it is because he remains imprisoned within himself.
Moreover, the scrupulous person is incapable of
letting himself be completely carried away by the
unquestionable evidence of values. He is always
seeking a further guarantee than the one provided
by his own insight into the value at stake. The man
who is truly awakened to his responsibility, on the
contrary, remains undecided only so long as he feels
he does not fully understand the claims of the value
at stake. But when this certainly is reached, he feels
himself secure and free.

Awareness of responsibility is a basic attitude for a religious concept of the world. The responsible man knows that he is not ruled only by an impersonal world of values, but a personal Judge, who is, at the same time the Sum of all values, and to whom he will have some day to render an account. Consequently, this attitude, like reverence, is a basis for all religion. Its significance, like that of reverence, constancy, or fidelity, extends to every domain of life, and is needed for all true knowledge, for all community life, for all artistic accomplishment, but above all for moral life, for a genuine moral personality, for the proper relationship of creatures to the Creator. Thus one of the main aims of all education and personality formation must be to lead to a fuller awareness of our responsibility.

Four

VERACITY

Truthfulness is another of the basic presuppositions for a person's moral life. An untruthful or mendacious person not only embodies a great moral disvalue, as does the avaricious or intemperate man, but he is crippled in his *whole* personality; the *whole* of his moral life; everything in him which is morally positive is threatened by his untruthfulness, and even becomes doubtful. His position toward the world of values as a whole, is affected at its very core.

The untruthful man lacks reverence toward values. He assumes a lordly position over being, he deals with it as he pleases, and treats it as if it were a mere chimera, a plaything of his arbitrary pleasure. He denies recognition and response to the value which inheres in being as such, to the dignity which being possesses by its opposition to nothingness. The untruthful person does not fulfill the fundamental obligation to recognize everything that

47

exists in its reality, not to interpret black as white, and not to deny a fact. He behaves toward being as if it did not exist. Obviously, this attitude implies an element of arrogance, of irreverence and impertinence. To treat another person "as if he were air," to act as if this man did not exist, is perhaps the greatest evidence of disrespect and contempt. The untruthful person takes this attitude toward the world of being. A madman disregards being as being because he does not grasp it. The untruthful man grasps it as such, but refuses the response which is due to the dignity and value of being simply because it is inconvenient or disagreeable for him to do so. His disregard of being is a conscious, guilty one.

A liar considers the whole world, to a certain extent, as but an instrument for his own ends; everything which exists is but an instrument for him; when he cannot use it, then he will deal with it as non-existent and place it in this category.

One must distinguish three different kinds of untruthfulness. First of all, in the artful liar who sees nothing wrong in affirming the contrary of what is true when it is expedient for his aims. Here we are dealing with a man who clearly and consciously cheats and betrays other men in order to reach his aims, like Iago in Shakespeare's *Othello*, or Franz Moor in Schiller's *Robbers*—though we also find in these two men a specific viciousness of intention which is not necessarily found in every liar. There also exist liars whose aims are less vicious.

The second type is that of the man who lies to himself and consequently to others. He is the man who simply erases from his mind everything in his life which is difficult or disagreeable, and who not only hides his head like an ostrich, but who persuades himself that he is going to do something, when he knows full well that he cannot do it. This is the man who does not want to recognize his own faults; he is the man who immediately twists the meaning of every situation which is humiliating or disagreeable for him so that it loses its sting. The difference which is to be found between an untruthful person of this type and the hypocrite or the artful liar is evident. His deception is above all practiced upon *himself*, and only indirectly upon others. He first deceives himself, and then cheats other men, half in good faith. He does not possess that consciousness of aim, that clarity which is proper to the liar, and in general, he lacks the wickedness and cunning meanness of the liar. In most cases he arouses our compassion. Yet, he is not without guilt, for he refuses the response due to values and to the dignity of being, and arrogates to himself a sovereignty over being which does not belong to him. Of course, he does not have the specific impertinence toward truth of the first type of liar; some remaining respect for truth prevents him from conscious and open neglect and distortion of truth. He fears to take this responsibility; he has not the courage of the hypocrite. By self-deceit he eludes the conflict between his inclinations and respect for truth. There is something specifically cowardly and feeble in his nature. In him the cunning and conscious artfulness of the liar is replaced by a more instinctive slyness.

The real liar is aware of the fact that he lies. He knows that he is ignoring reality. The untruthful person, living in self-deception, denies to himself the very fact that he is ignoring the truth in question. It is just because he distorts and misinterprets the facts that when he lies he is unaware of a conflict with truth.

In spite of the fact that this type of liar is generally less wicked (although a form of this un-

truthfulness exists also in the Pharisee, who does
not see the beam in his own eye, and who is wicked
in the deepest sense), and that usually he is less
responsible, yet the consequences of his untruthfulness, are for his entire moral life, immense. One
can no longer take this type of person seriously. His
moral action may be right in individual cases where
the response to value does not involve conflict either
with his pride or his concupiscence. But as soon as
something disagreeable is required of him, though
he does not consciously defy the call of values, he
will elude it. He will take refuge in the illusion that,
for one reason or another, this demand does not
hold good for him, or that the demand is only an
apparent one, or that he has already complied with
this demand. The inner life of such men resembles
quicksand; one cannot get hold of them; they always elude one's grasp. Even though a conscious
liar is, morally speaking, still more reprehensible,
a conversion can more easily be brought about in
him than in these self-deceivers. For these latter the
inner life is affected by a greater sickness; in them
evil has taken possession of a psychologically
deeper level. They live in a world of illusion. Nevertheless, the untruthfulness of such men carries its

share of guilt; for it could be abolished by a basic inner conversion of the will, by not shrinking from sacrifice, and by unconditional abandonment to the world of values.

In the third type of untruthfulness, the break with truth is still less reprehensible, but goes perhaps still deeper, and is reflected even more in the very being of its perpetrators. We see it in that type of ungenuine persons whose personality is a deception, who are incapable of experiencing real joy, genuine enthusiasm, genuine love, whose every attitude is a sham, and bears the stamp of pretence. These men do not want to deceive and dupe others; neither do they wish to cheat themselves, but they are unable to achieve a real and genuine contact with the world. The reason for this is that they are enclosed within themselves, always twisting their gaze back upon themselves, and in so doing they destroy the inner substance of their attitudes. The fault does not lie in their distortion of being, in their unresponsiveness to its dignity, but in a general self-centeredness which takes away the inner life of their responses, and makes their personality into a sham.

They are those shadowlike beings who are un-

genuine; even though their intention is honest, their
joys and sorrows are artificial. Their untruthfulness is due to the fact that all their attitudes are
not really motivated by the object and are not en-
flamed by contact with it, but are artificially stimu-
lated; they pretend to conform to the object, but in
reality they are only phantoms without substance.

This lack of genuineness can manifest itself in
different ways; it can, above all, assume different
dimensions. It is proper, first, to the affected person
whose exterior behavior although not actually sim-
ulated, is unnatural, artificial and untrue. It is
proper, secondly, to those people easily influenced
by suggestion, whose opinions and convictions are
imposed on them by others, and who only reaffirm
what others have said without ever being truly determined by the object involved. Thirdly, it is
proper to the exaggerated person who works himself up in all things, in his sorrow, in his joy, in his
love, in his hatred, in his enthusiasm; he fosters
these artificially because he relishes himself in those
attitudes.

Ungenuineness as found in the three last-men-
tioned types is still less wicked than it is in him who
deceives himself, but a moral life cannot be based

on such a foundation. For everything, good as well as bad, is rendered invalid by such an artificial attitude. It makes everything unreal, everything but a sham, a nothingness. This substantial untruthfulness is also culpable because it stems from an ultimate refusal to abandon oneself to values, from a basic attitude of pride.

The man who is really truthful is opposed to the three above-mentioned types of untruthfulness. He is genuine, he cheats neither himself nor other people. Because of his deep reverence for the majesty of being, he understands the basic demand of the value which inheres in every being. (I mean by this demand the obligation of paying tribute to every thing that exists, of conforming to truth in all our assertions, of refraining from building up a world of sham and nothingness.) He takes into account the metaphysical situation of man, which grants him no omnipotence so that being must yield to his wishes as if it were a mere chimera, i.e. he takes truth into account not only with regard to individual things and conditions which present themselves to his mind, but also with regard to his attitude as a man in the world. He understands the value which inheres in truth, and the negative value of lies,

of falsity and of inner revolt against the world of
values (and in the last account against God, the
Absolute Being, the Lord of all being) which is con-
tained in every untruth. He understands the responsibility which man as a spiritual person has in
regard to truth, and which is to be found in man's
power to depict being in an assertion made by him.
He understands the solemnity inherent in every
affirmation, for in making an affirmation one is
called upon to be a witness to truth. The truthful
person places the demands of values above every
subjective wish prompted by his selfishness or his
comfort. He consequently abhors all self-deception.
He sees the whole negative value of a cowardly flight
from the objective demands of the world of values.
He would rather know the most bitter truth than
enjoy an imaginary happiness. The whole pointless-
ness of every flight into a world of unreality is clear
to his eyes; he grasps the complete uselessness of
self-deception, the futility of this type of behavior,
the emptiness and shallowness of every untruth.

Finally, the truthful man who has a "classical"
relationship with being, is the man who in his every
attitude and action is genuine and true. In his soul
we do not find sham attitudes, he does not em-

bellish and puff up the experiences which he truly
has, he does not twist his gaze back on himself instead of looking at the object which demands a
response of him. He is the genuine and straight-
forward man, i.e. the objective man in the highest
sense of that word. He is the man who possesses in
his basic attitude true abandonment to values, and
who holds himself free from personal pride, so that
he is not moved to arrogate to himself a position in
the world other than the one which is objectively
due him. Thus he neither falsifies the import of an
experience, nor gives it another character than the
one it possesses in reality.

The truthful person does not seek compensation
for his inferiority complexes. The kinship which
finds its expression in the words, "Humility is
truth," may also be expressed conversely. The
humble person alone is really truthful. The source
of all ungenuineness and all untruthfulness is found
in the proud desire to be something different from
what we really are. The most profound assent given
to truth, to being, is the foundation for all genuineness and truthfulness. This is often misunderstood
in the sense that the pessimist, the skeptic, the man
who refuses to recognize any higher reality than the

palpable, or the fatalist who renounces all intervention in the world and who despairs of all progress and all development, are considered as especially truthful persons. To accept this would be a complete misunderstanding. Such persons give assent only to a segment of being, and never to its whole. They do not recognize the demand of the world of values or the promise of development, change, and elevation of one's own being which lies in this demand. They neglect the meaning of man and of the world which belongs as much to being as the stone we see lying on the ground and the air we breathe. Consequently, they are not completely truthful, for they give assent only to the superficial strata of being, and not to its deeper and more important strata. Yet transformation and development must take place within the framework of the person's own individuality and capacity,[1] i.e. they must be ontologically true and not consist in indulgence in illusion or a flight into fancy.

There exist manifold elements in the specific negative value of a lie, the classical example of untruthfulness. First of all, in such an affirmation

[1] Here, of course, I do not refer to moral transformation, which is always within the range of every man.

there is a revolt against the dignity of being as such, an irreverent arrogance, and disregard of the fundamental obligation to conform to being. To lie is to misuse the quality entrusted to us as witnesses to being, in speech, in the spoken or written word. Secondly, we must consider the deception of other men which is linked with a lie. To deceive another person implies a fundamental disrespect, a failure to take him seriously. It ignores the value which inheres in every man as a spiritual person, shows a disregard of the dignity of man, of the elementary right which every person possesses to know the truth. It shows, above all, a deep lack of charity and an abuse of the confidence which the other person reposes in us. These elements are to be found in every intentional deception practiced upon another, but, in a very special way, in a deception effected by means of a false affirmation, by a lie. For the communication by words, in its very form, implies an explicit "I-Thou" relationship; it appeals so expressly to the basic confidence of man in man, that the lack of charity and the betrayal of the other person, in this case, is still more striking and more telling than in the case of a deception by means of ambiguity, or misleading behavior.

Now, there are cases in which deception as such is permitted, nay, is commanded. For example, if a criminal is following us, it is permissible for us to deceive him, in one way or the other, about our dwelling-place. It is commanded when we could severely harm another person either physically or morally by communicating the truth. In the latter case, it is no lack of charity to deceive; on the contrary, it is a loving kindliness. Thus, we are permitted to deceive other persons in certain given cases; in others, we are obliged to do so. But we may do this only by means of silence, ambiguous expressions or behavior, by means of our interpretation of a given situation; never by means of a direct lie. For the negative value possessed by a lie (in the first place in the misuse of our duty as witnesses to truth and lack of reverence toward the dignity of being) is so great that no situation in the world can justify it. Even when kindness for another person forces us to deceive him, we must still abstain from doing so if the deception can be realized only by means of a lie.

Veracity is, like reverence, fidelity or constancy and the awareness of responsibility, a basis of our whole moral life. Like these other virtues, it bears a high value in itself, and like these is also indispensable as a basic presupposition of a personality in which genuine moral values may flower in their plenitude. This proves true in all the domains of life. Veracity is the basis for all true community life, for every relationship of person to person, for every true love, for every profession, for true knowledge, for self-education, and for the relationship of men to God. Yes, a basic element of veracity is, in a specific way, its relationship to the absolute Source of all being, God. For, in the last account, untruthfulness means a denial of God, a flight from Him. An education which does not lay emphasis on truthfulness and veracity, condemns itself to failure.

Five

GOODNESS

Goodness is the very heart of the whole reign of moral values. It is by no accident that the term "good" means moral value as such, and also the specific moral quality of goodness. Among the different moral values there is none which embodies more completely the entire reign of moral values, than goodness; in it we find the purest and most typical expression of the general character of moral goodness as such. It is the center of all morality, and at the same time, its most sublime fruit. Its central importance in the moral sphere is, therefore, of a completely different type from that of the fundamental attitudes previously mentioned: reverence, fidelity, awareness of responsibility and veracity. For, apart from their own high moral value, these virtues are accepted as a presupposition for the moral life. Goodness, on the contrary, is not a presupposition, but the fruit of moral life. But not a fruit among others, such as meekness, patience, gen-

erosity, but the fruit of fruits, i.e. that in which cul-
minates all morality in a specific way; it is the
queen of all virtues.

What is goodness? What do we mean when we
say that a man irradiates goodness? We say this of
a man when he is disposed to help, when he is
kindly, just, when he is ready to make sacrifices for
others, when he pardons wrongs done him, when
he is generous, when he is full of compassion. All
these qualities are specific forms and manifestations
of love. This indicates the close connection which
exists between love and goodness. Love is, as it were,
flowing goodness, and goodness is the breath of
love.

We have seen at the beginning that the whole
moral life consists in meaningful responses to
values which have been grasped, such responses as
enthusiasm, admiration, joy, obedience, love. But
love is, among all these responses to values, the
most complete and the deepest. First of all, one
must realize that love is always a most outspoken
response to value. When we love somebody, whether
it be a friend, a parent, a child, whether it be con-
jugal love or neighborly love, the beloved person
always stands before us as something precious and

noble in himself. As long as someone is merely agreeable to us or only useful for our purposes, we could not love him. This does not mean that we become blind to the faults of the beloved person. But the person as a whole must stand before us as endowed with a sublime value and filled with intrinsic preciousness; yes, that specific individuality which every man represents as a unique thought of God must reveal itself before our eyes in all its charm and beauty, if we are to love him.

Love is always a response to value. In love, one responds not only with a specific word, but with the gift of one's heart, with oneself. In love, one conspires with value more closely and more deeply than in any other response, such as, for example, reverence or obedience. In love, a man dwells in the values of the beloved, in a completely different way. Love, in its fullest and proper meaning, addresses itself always to persons, or at least to nonpersonal entities which we treat as personal (as, for example, one's country). There are responses to values which are directed toward things, attitudes, and events, as well as toward persons, as for example, joy, sorrow, enthusiasm. Other responses to values from their very nature address themselves only to persons, as veneration, gratitude, confidence, obedience and love. In the response of love to the other person two fundamental elements are manifested. The affirmation of the being of the beloved one, the abandoning response to his intrinsic beauty unfolds itself, on the one hand, in a longing to participate in his being, to be united with him; and on the other hand, in the will to bestow happiness on him.

In love, one spiritually hastens toward the other person in order to dwell with him, to partake in him, and, on the other hand, to cover him with a mantle of goodness, to spiritually cherish and protect him. Every love which deserves the name of love possesses these two elements, even though in a specific love, one or the other element will prevail.

The second element, namely, an ultimate interest in the growth and unfoldment of the beloved, in his perfection and his happiness, and in the last account, in his salvation, this envelopment of the beloved in love, is, as we have already said, pure flowing goodness. Here we find goodness in its purest manifestation. Goodness always presupposes a special attitude toward other persons, even to beings of a lower order possessing a certain analogy to

persons, such as animals; thus, it is contradistin-
guished from truthfulness, which responds to the
value of being as such. We say "attitude of response
to value toward persons in general," for the goodness of a man does not limit itself to benevolent in
tentions toward one particular person whom one
loves. When we say someone is good, we mean that
he continually manifests this open benevolence, that
his attitude toward every man has, *a priori*, this loving, this generous character. For goodness, like
every other virtue, is not limited to a particular
momentary attitude, but it is a property of man, a
part of his superactual being, a basic attitude and
position.

There are three types of men who embody a
specific antithesis to goodness: the indifferent or
cold man, the hardhearted one, and the wicked
one. The latter is the man who is an enemy of
values: the man who is ruled by a basic attitude
of pride, and who lives in an impotent revolt against
the world of values. He not only bluntly by-passes
them, as does the sensual man, but he assails them;
he would like to dethrone God, he hates the world
of goodness and beauty, and all the world of light,
like Alberich in the *Nibelungenring* of Richard

Wagner. He is full of envy and rebellion against
the world of values, and against every good and
happy man. He is the man like Cain, who feeds
himself upon hatred. His attitude toward other men
not only lacks kindliness, but is expressly hostile.
He wants to hurt his fellowmen, and to wound them
with the poison of his hatred. I do not refer to the
misanthrope who, having been disillusioned, is at
war with humanity as a whole and every individual
person; he has rather turned away from mankind
than turned against it; this type is more tragic than
wicked. I am thinking of the malicious man who
would like to pour out his poison everywhere, like
Iago in Shakespeare's *Othello*, or Pizarro in
Beethoven's *Fidelio*. A specific variety of this type
is the fundamentally cruel man, who enjoys the
sufferings of others. Instead of the luminous harmony of goodness, we find here a somber dis-
harmony; instead of the warm diffusing rays of
happiness and life radiated by love, one finds
virulent and lacerating hatred; instead of clear,
free affirmation, one finds a destroying search for
nothingness, a being imprisoned in a spasm of
negation.

We find another antithesis to goodness in the

hardhearted person. He is the stern, cold man who
is never moved by compassion, whose ear is deaf to
all petitions, who tramples on everything without
consideration, and for whom other men are mere
figures placed on the chessboard of his plans. He is
not a deliberate enemy of other people, but completely hard and uncharitable. In no way does this
type take into account the natures of other men as
spiritual persons, as sensitive and vulnerable
creatures. He ignores their rights and claims as personal beings; he treats them as if they were mere
objects. He represents a classical type of the pure
egoist. He reminds us of certain slave-dealers, or
of Landvogt Gessler in Schiller's *William Tell*. Instead of the inner freedom of the charitable man,
we find in him an inner compression and hardening
of the heart. In place of openness and accessibility
to his fellowmen, we find him closed in upon himself and impenetrable. Instead of response to the
positive value of the other's happiness and the
negative value of his suffering, we find refusal of
any response; instead of solidarity with the other
person (i.e. the capacity to transcend oneself in
order to suffer and rejoice with others), we find
total imprisonment in self, an icy and brutal gaze

looking beyond others. Instead of the victorious,
selfless superiority of the man who is at the service
of all, and never seeks anything for himself, we find
the inferiority of the brutal superman, and instead
of generous forgiveness of injustices suffered, we
find relentless vengeance.

Finally, the antithesis to the good man is the
cold, indifferent man. He is the man who by-passes
his fellowmen with a blighting lack of comprehension; the man who lives for his own comforts
and enjoyments; he, too, is a typical egoist, but he
has a different complexion from the hardhearted
man. He is neither hostile toward others, nor
brutally and unrelentingly hard, but he is filled
with indifference toward his fellowmen. He may be
moved by fearful sights, he experiences disgust and
horror when facing illness, he cannot bear the sight
of blood, but all this is but a nervous reaction to an
aesthetically shocking object. For he flees from
awful sights and seeks pleasant scenes, while the
good man hastens to help.

On the other hand, this type of man is even more
cold than the hardhearted man. The hardhearted
man, it is true, has an icy coldness, he does not know
the voice of the heart; he is heartless. Yet he does

know the fire of hatred, the cold burning of vengeance, of rage. He is not indifferent. He is not invulnerable. He is familiar with the irritation caused by offenses and humiliations, but he does not know what it means to be wounded to the heart by lack of charity, injustice, and, above all, by the sufferings of our fellowmen, and other objective negative values.

The indifferent man, on the contrary, has not the sternness and brutality of the hardhearted man; he cannot even be pierced by insults; only that which is disagreeable and uncomfortable bothers him. He is not a superman like the hardhearted man; he may even be an aesthete. He is unable to share other people's feelings, for he is much too occupied with his own concerns. He is not only selfish, he is above all egocentric, i.e. he is occupied with his own feelings and moods, and his gaze is centered upon himself. The whole world is there only for his satisfaction. He is therefore incapable of deeper inward emotions; in the end everything leaves him indifferent. Instead of the warmth and ardor of the good man, empty neutrality and cool indifference reign here. We find here no inner riches or inner fecundity, only sterile poverty and fruitless emptiness.

Instead of the awakedness and openness of the good man, we find him circumscribed and blind regarding values, and instead of the all-embracing breadth of the good man we find in him a petty narrowness.

Thus we see the fundamental features of goodness. Luminous harmony, inner freedom and serenity, the victorious superiority of love—which is the secret of eager and ready service—openness to the life of other men, warmth, ardor, meekness and mildness, all-embracing breadth, awakedness, and the capacity to grasp values. It is above all important to understand that goodness, although it is tender and meek, possesses at the same time the greatest strength. Faced with its irresistible power, with its superior security and freedom, the force of the superman is only miserable weakness and childish pretence. One should not mistake goodness for weak surrender, a surrender without resistance. The truly good man can be immovable when one tries to divert him from the right path, and when the salvation of his neighbor calls imperatively for sternness. He unshakably resists every seduction and temptation.

One should beware of confusing goodness with good-nature. The good-natured man is harmless and

is an appeaser; because of a certain lassitude and
inertia of his nature, he lets himself be badly
treated without noticing it. His amiable attitude
has its source in a completely unconscious tendency
of his nature. Goodness, on the contrary, flows from
a conscious response of love; it is "ardent awakedness" and never "harmless lassitude." It is the most
intensive moral life, and not inertia and dullness;
it is strength and not weakness. The good man does
not allow himself to be made use of because he
lacks the strength to resist, but he serves freely
and humbles himself willingly.

In goodness there shines a light which bestows
on the good person an especial intellectual dignity.
The truly good man is never stupid and narrow,
even though he may be slow intellectually, and not
gifted for intellectual activities. The man who is
not good, in any of the fore-mentioned ways, is, in
the last account, always limited, even stupid. This
is true even if he has produced works of great intellectual power. Goodness, the breath and fra-
grance of love, is the essence of every truly moral
life, yes, of every true life of the soul. Whereas the
other fundamental attitudes, such as reverence,
faithfulness, awareness of responsibility and ve-

racity respond to the world of values as a whole, goodness not only responds to this world of values, but is, so to speak, the reflection of the whole world of values in the person. Goodness speaks in the voice and in the name of this world.

What has been said of love applies to goodness as well: "He who does not love abides in death." In its mysterious strength it shakes the world to its very foundations; it bears on its forehead the sign of victory over wickedness and disorder, over all hatred and all unfeeling coarseness.